A Tale of Three Ships:

Setting Sail for Your Extraordinary Dream

Inspirations for Creating the Life You Want

bright sky press

2365 Rice Boulevard, Suite 202,
Houston, Texas 77005

10 9 8 7 6 5 4 3 2

Edwards, Dwight, 1954-
A tale of three ships : setting sail for your extraordinary dream :
inspirations for creating the life you want / Dwight Edwards.
p. cm.
ISBN 978-1-933979-59-5 (hardcover)
1. Self-realization. 2. Quality of life. 3. Conduct of life. I. Title.

BJ1470.E38 2009
170'.44–dc22   2009028204

Illustrations by Mike Guillory
Printed in China through Asia Pacific Offset

A Tale of Three Ships:
Setting Sail for Your Extraordinary Dream

Inspirations for Creating the Life You Want

DWIGHT EDWARDS

bright sky press

HOUSTON, TEXAS

To Stephen, Jordan, and Brandon —
the finest sons a dad could ever hope for.
I am so proud of each of you. May you each discover
your extraordinary dream and set sail for it!

Table of Contents

INTRODUCTION

> *"The unexamined life is not worth living."*
> — **Socrates**

La Nina, La Pinta, y La Santa Maria. I don't remember much of what I learned in Mrs. Lizarraga's fourth grade Spanish class, but she made sure these three ships of Christopher Columbus would always be a part of me. Memorizing them was your only option if you wanted to avoid her wrath or possibly a rerun of her class.

And if you were adventurous enough to be part of Columbus' first journey to the New World, these three ships likewise were your only option. For a period of seven months, one of these three would determine the direction you headed, the quality of life you experienced, and the particular work you contributed. The boat you sailed on would be far more than a protection from the ocean's waters. It would be your worksite, your community, your home, and, in large measure, your identity. And so it is today.

As we journey across life's waters, it seems to me that

we are each given the option of three possible ships to sail upon. Three, and only three. The sinking ship, the cruise ship, or the battleship. While Columbus chose which ship each of his eighty-seven men would be assigned to, we have the freedom and privilege to determine which boat will be ours. But along with this freedom come the consequences and rewards of our choice. It behooves us then to choose wisely.

And that's what this book is all about. It's a close examination of each available ship — understanding what they offer, where they are headed, and what their lasting significance will be. Most of all, it is about choosing wisely while there is still time to choose.

Before we begin looking at each ship, let me quickly describe what I hope you, the reader, will get out of this work. First, I hope this book will lead to **_deep reflection_**. It is so desperately easy in our fast-paced, frenetic culture to put our heads down and keep charging ahead, tragically unaware of all that is passing us by as we spend our days in the trenches of relentless activity. As poet T. S. Eliot put it, _"Where is the Life we have lost in living?"_ Every now and then it is critical to come out of the trenches, take a good look around, and then make the necessary adjustments before going back in.

When was the last time you took some significant time off to carefully scrutinize where your life is heading and the ways you would like for it to be different? I hope this book will help you do this. Let me encourage you, then, to read it slowly…leaving plenty of time for reflection and meditation.

Secondly, I hope this book will lead to **deep encouragement**. Some of you have lost hope that anything significant will ever come of your life. You feel trapped in a cage of daily responsibilities, and your soul is dying a slow death of vanilla poisoning. Nothing about your life is extraordinary, and there seems little chance of that changing anytime soon.

Oh, how I would love to reach inside of you and turn the lights back on! To help you see the part that you alone are to play and to help you discover that unique work created solely for you and you for it. And how I would enjoy seeing your face light up from the deepseated satisfaction of your soul having come home to what it was made for, be it great or small in this world's eyes. If this book could help, even in a small way, to that end, it will all have been worth it.

Just a word as you read — don't ever, ever, ever give up on yourself. You have more to offer than you have any idea; and no past failures are big enough or numerous enough to exclude you from mighty living in the days ahead. I wholly agree with the words of John Gardner, prolific author and former secretary of education, "*There is something I know about you that you may not even know about yourself. You have within you more resources of energy than have ever been tapped, more talent than has ever been exploited, more strength than has ever been tested, and more to give than you have ever given.*" He's right, you know.

Finally, my desire is that this book will lead to **deep commitment**. That you will gain a clearer vision of your extraordinary dream (to be explained later), allow it to possess you, to enflame you, and finally to launch you unreservedly into the unpredictable but adventurous seas of dream fulfillment. And that, like Columbus, you will hoist your anchors and set sail for a new world. A new world of no longer living for others' approval, a new world of boldly releasing that which is deepest within you, a new world of risking yourself on a daily basis, a new world of living passionately from your truest and deepest center. Your soul will never be fully satisfied with anything less.

But this "new-world" living costs deeply and costs frequently. And it will require a deep commitment or we will never persevere through the storms and setbacks that inevitably come with the territory.

I believe God has given each of us something vitally unique to contribute to the world. There is a song only you can sing, a poem only you can write, a niche only you can fill, and an influence that you and you alone can exert. No one can step in and read your script for you, or serve as your understudy in life. Your short stay on this planet is meant to leave it a different place than when you arrived. You matter…not only because of who you are, but especially because of what you have to offer this needy, broken world. I plead with you on behalf of this world's inhabitants: Don't rob us of what you uniquely have to offer. Give us your deepest best.

Columbus almost never made it. Two months into the journey his crew came within a hair's breadth of mutinying and turning back. They were panic-stricken by the belief that soon they would fall off the end of the earth.

On October 9, 1492, Columbus promised that the expedition would turn back if they didn't see evidence of land within three days. At 2 a.m., three days later, the Pinta's lookout Rodrigo de Triana cried out, "Tierra! Tierra!" (Land! Land!). And the rest, as they say, is history.

What will your history be? How will the captain's log of your ship read when it is all said and done? The good news is that it is yet to be determined. Adjustments can still be made, new voyages can still be undertaken, new vistas can still be opened up. There is no need to turn back.

One person may have several extraordinary dreams in a lifetime, while another has but one. Our dreams, like our fingerprints, will vary from one individual to another. The great issue is not finding a dream of grandiose proportions, but finding that dream (or dreams) which makes you most alive as a human being. That dream will call you by name, will hold you in its clutches, will very possibly scare you to death, but also excite you to the core. And it is a dream which enables you to say at the end of the day, "I know, but know, that this is what I was made for."

This dream I am speaking of is far more than wishful thinking or a mildly good idea. Throughout history, the dreams of extraordinary risk-takers have contained three central elements: vision, passion and action. Or to put it another way, it is a dream that profoundly influences the head, the heart and the hand.

Vision — This dream boldly and specifically envisions the details of what could be with clear specifics.

Not necessarily all the specifics, but enough to mightily captivate the mind with unrealized possibilities. Walt Disney died a few years before the completion of his Walt Disney World Resort dream project in Florida. Following its dedication, two Disney executives were talking. One said, "Too bad Uncle Walt wasn't here to see this." To which the other replied, "Oh, but he did see it, that's why it is here." As Walt Disney said, *"If you can dream it, you can do it. Always remember that this whole thing was started with a dream and a mouse."*

Passion — This dream possesses not only the head but also the heart. It is not only informed but also enflamed. It is characterized by an image in the mind and a fire in the bones. It is a fairly reliable rule of thumb: If your dream does not ignite you internally, you probably have not yet found that dream you were made for. *"When you discover your mission, you will feel its demand. It will fill you with enthusiasm and a burning desire to get to work on it,"* wrote best-selling author W. Clement Stone.

Action — The final characteristic of this dream is that it inevitably translates into action. There is substantial sweat equity required for any worthwhile vision to become reality. The extraordinary dream is not merely wishful thinking or heightened emotion. It is resolute action at the cost of time, sweat, and energy. As Thomas Edison once quipped, *"Opportunity is missed by most people because it is dressed in overalls and looks like work."* Your dream won't look like work, it *will* be work. But work that will bring a vitality to your life and a satisfaction to your soul that you will find nowhere else.

Let me invite you, then, to climb up into the crow's nest and begin the exploration. My hope is that you too will catch sight of a land that beckons you by name, that entices you out of your comfort zone, and leads you to a quality and significance of life you only dreamed of. Your life was meant to be extraordinary, your days upon this planet were meant to count. May that be your history, may that be your captain's log. Come, my friend, let's set sail...

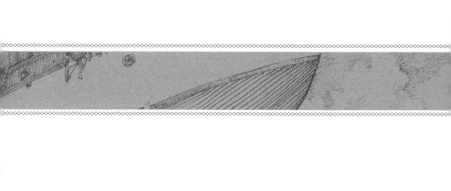

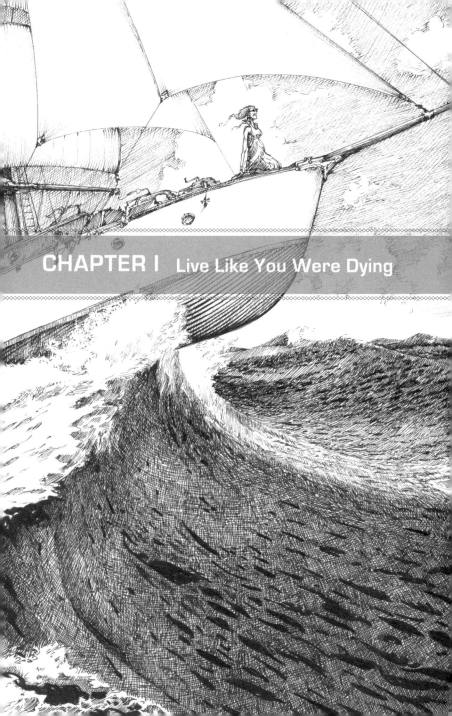

CHAPTER I   Live Like You Were Dying

It was the most startling news he had ever read. Not often does a person find out about their death while they are still living, but such was the case of Swedish chemist Alfred Nobel.

One morning while vacationing in France, he opened the newspaper and glanced upon the headline, "Alfred Nobel Dies." Deciding this story was definitely worth reading, he discovered through the article how he had died the night before. What actually happened was that his brother, Ludwig, had passed away unexpectedly and an overzealous French reporter had hastily written the article to make the deadline for the morning paper. Unfortunately, he hadn't properly researched which Nobel it was who died.

But the article devastated Alfred. Earlier in his life he had invented dynamite and through his patent had amassed a huge fortune. It was always his intent that this explosive be used to aid mankind (building roads, constructing tunnels, etc.). But in the article he found himself referred to as "inventor of destruction" and "merchant of death." Realizing that this was the legacy he would be remembered for, he made a critical decision which would forever salvage how people thought of the name Nobel.

He took the vast majority of his fortune and placed it into a fund for the betterment of mankind. His biographer writes, "...*it* (the mistaken article) *pained him so much he never forgot it. Indeed, he became so obsessed with his posthumous reputation that he rewrote his last will, bequeathing most of his fortune to a cause which no future obituary written would be able to cast aspersions.*" That cause, that fund, is known today as the Nobel Prizes and one of the six is the Nobel Peace Prize! And a mistaken article was exactly the reason it came into being.

What a strange but fortunate turn of events for Dr. Nobel. Because he was given the unexpected opportunity to know beforehand what he would be remembered for after his death, he was able to change his life's course and carve out for himself a noble (no pun intended) and enduring legacy. And he serves forever as a monument to the power and possibilities of a re-charted life.

Yet, Dr. Nobel serves not only as a monument but also as a mentor. Every one of us can gain tremendous benefit and wisdom from his course alteration. You see, we are all charting a course in life, whether we are aware of it or not. We are all in the process of being remembered for something, like it or not. Our sails are hoisted, the winds are blowing, and our life is heading somewhere.

The only question is where. And before it is too late we all need to carefully evaluate the route our ship is taking. Socrates was exactly right when he said so many years ago, "*The unexamined life is not worth living.*"

But how does one do that? Strange and morbid as it may sound, I know of no better way than carefully envisioning one's own funeral. A good means for doing this is to ask ourselves, "If I were to die today, what would be said about me at my funeral? And even more importantly, what would I *like* to be said?"

Ever really think about it? Ever consider actually jotting down on paper the exact things you hope will be said about you at your last formal remembrance? Pretty heavy stuff, eh? But such, such important stuff. You could write your obituary now and keep it updated as life goes on and you have more successes. No one knows better than you what you want said and written about you when you die. The weightiness of this activity can do you a tremendous favor in provoking a new evaluation concerning the direction your life is heading and the legacy you are in the process of leaving.

Like Alfred Nobel, it can serve as the catalyst which changes your course of living. Or equally, it may be your confirmation to stay the course you are already on. Either way, writing out specifically what you would like to be remembered for at your funeral can catapult you into a renewed and refocused urgency to live life at full throttle in a significant direction. It helps us, in the words of singer Tim McGraw, "*…to live like you were dying.*"

Steve Jobs explained in a commencement speech at

Stanford University in 2005 how important this principle of living in light of death has been to him, "*Remembering that I'll be dead soon is the most important tool I've ever encountered to help me make the big choices in life. Because almost everything — all external expectations, all pride, all fear of embarrassment or failure — these things just fall away in the face of death, leaving only what is truly important. Remembering that you are going to die is the best way I know to avoid the trap of thinking you have something to lose. You are already naked. There is no reason not to follow your heart.*" Not only does the reality of death affect how we live in the present, it also impacts what we want to be remembered for once we are gone.

John is the head golf pro at one of this nation's most exclusive country clubs. He makes a very comfortable living, works in a very comfortable setting, and, frankly, is envied by almost all the surrounding golf pros. He told me recently, though, that none of these things are really doing the job of satisfying that deepest part within him which yearns to know his life has counted for something genuinely significant. "Dwight," he said, "Last Sunday I was working with a member, helping him with his putting. And in the middle of the lesson it suddenly struck me that if I were to die right now, I would probably be best remembered as someone who helped golfers improve their game. That's *not* what I want to be best remembered for." And this realization has launched him into a renewed focus and pursuit of the kinds of things he does want to be remembered for.

Now this is not to say that helping people improve in

their sport is an insignificant goal. Far from it. Coaching is a tremendous occupation and a very worthwhile pursuit. The question my friend was wrestling with (as we all need to) is what things exactly do we want to be *most* remembered for as a result of our few, short years on this earth? What course of life is most worth charting and sailing? That is what this book is all about.

A Tale of Three Ships. This is an extended parable about what I believe to be humanity's three main approaches to life. It is a description of the kind of course each ship is charting, the quality of life each offers, and the kind of legacy each leaves in its wake. In these pages you will witness the saga of the sinking ship, the cruise ship, and the battleship. And you will come to understand and appreciate more fully the words of author Jack London when he summarized his philosophy of life in these stirring words:

"*I would rather be ashes than dust! I would rather that my spark should burn out in a brilliant blaze than it should be stifled by dry-rot. I would rather be a superb meteor, every atom of me in magnificent glow, than a sleepy and permanent planet. The function of man is to live, not to exist. I shall not waste my days trying to prolong them. I shall use my time.*"

Is that not what you and I really want as well? Of course it is. What keeps us then from this white-hot approach to life? Maybe we have unwittingly boarded the wrong ship. Let's check it out.

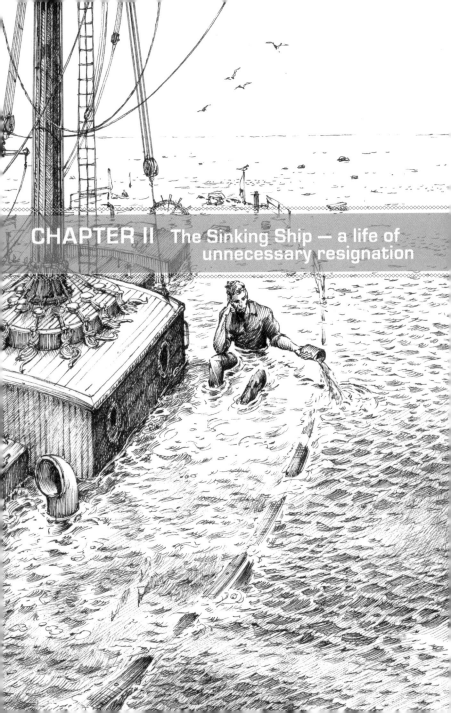

CHAPTER II The Sinking Ship — a life of unnecessary resignation

> *"Most men lead lives of quiet desperation and go to the grave with the song still in them."*
>
> **– Henry David Thoreau**

On a sinking ship everyone has one supreme, over-riding goal — *survival*. Watch the movie *Titanic*, and you will see that once this mighty ship begins going under, everyone's primary pursuit becomes the same. The people on the lower decks want up, the people on top want in the lifeboats, and everyone is frantically searching for a way that they and their loved ones can escape the watery grave of the Atlantic Ocean. There are times in life when survival becomes our loftiest goal. Survival… in its many different forms.

For many, many people daily physical survival is the highest pursuit of their existence. On the average day about one-seventh of the world's population (852 million) goes to bed hungry and malnourished. 1.2 billion people (about one-fifth of the world's population) live beneath the international poverty line — making less than one dollar per day. For these individuals and many more, making physical survival the primary goal of their lives is really their only option. Until the basic needs for physical survival are met, people are not going to be concerned about doing something extraordinary with their lives.

In Abraham Maslow's famous hierarchy of human needs, he notes this very thing: "*Undoubtedly these physiological needs are the most pre-potent of all needs.*" A man who is bleeding from a gunshot wound has little concern as to whether or not his boss will praise him for his last project.

Sometimes grief survival is the most pressing goal of all. Edna St. Vincent Millay described this powerfully in her poem, "Lament", in which she reminds us that life must go on, and we forget about the dead. Even though good men have died. Anne must eat her breakfast and Dan must take his medicine:

"*Life must go on; I forget just why.*"

For all of us, there will be times that survival (in its many different forms) will be the highest goal we can muster. Whether it be financial survival, emotional survival, relational survival or job survival, we all have periods where we are bleeding profusely from the wounds this world inflicts upon us. During those times, living life at full-throttle means simply being able to get out of bed, to put one foot in front of the other, and to make it through one day (often one hour) at a time. There are periods in our life when survival is a monumental feat.

My concern is not for those times, however. It is for choosing to make survival the central theme of one's entire life when circumstances do not require it. Many people on this planet have their daily, physical needs taken care of. Perhaps not wants, but needs. They are in the position of being able to launch out into deeper waters and do something extraordinary with their lives. Yet, for whatever reason, they choose to play defense all their days. Their highest aspiration is the careful maintenance of risk-free living and a comfortable-as-possible existence. The word that best summarizes their existence is *resignation*. Resigned to simply getting by, resigned to never pursuing one's highest dreams, resigned to playing safe, resigned to rice-cake living. As poet and naturalist Henry David Thoreau put it, "*The mass of men lead lives of quiet desperation. What is called resignation is confirmed desperation.*"

What do I mean by survival? Let me give you three of the most prominent types of survival people face. Beyond physical survival there is *financial survival* — working to be sure that all the bills are paid and money is being stored away for the future. Now, I am in no way downplaying the importance of making and saving money. Obviously this is a critical and inevitable part of life. And the pressures can be immense. But the problem arises when money maintenance becomes one's all-consuming focus in life, and thereby ends up slowly robbing a man or woman of the wide-eyed adventure of living out their highest calling. Scoutmaster and writer

Forest Whitcraft expressed it well, "*A hundred years from now it will not matter what my bank account was, the sort of house I lived in, or the kind of car I drove...but the world may be different because I was important in the life of a child.*"

Many a life has been put on hold indefinitely while the person waits until they are a little better off. Problem is, better off usually never comes. Yes, there are bills to be paid. Yes, there are expenses to be met. Yes, there are monthly mortgage payments due. But is this all there is to life? Is this the cause, as important and necessary as it is, we want to have at the forefront of our existence? Does anyone really desire the highest eulogy of their funeral to be, "He or she handled their money responsibly"? Of course not. But if our overriding goal in life is merely financial survival, this is the legacy we are in danger of leaving.

There also is ***emotional survival***. Here the great goal of life is to keep one's heart intact or at least carefully shielded from significant hurt. Given the abuse in many people's backgrounds, this is a very understandable goal. But a guarded life is never a vibrant life, and when no one can touch us deeply, an essential part of our humanity has been laid to rest. This approach to life is expressed powerfully by C. S. Lewis in *The Four Loves:*

"*To love at all is to be vulnerable. Love anything, and your heart will certainly be wrung and possibly broken. If you want to make sure of keeping it intact, you must give your heart to no one, not even to an animal. Wrap it carefully round with hobbies and little luxuries; avoid all entanglements; lock it up safe in the casket or coffin of your selfishness. But in the casket-safe, dark, motionless, airless — it will change. It will not be broken; it will become unbreakable, impenetrable, irredeemable."*

When emotional survival becomes our primary goal in life, we become a rock, an island; we touch no one, and no one touches us. And we go to our graves with a rubberized heart, a guarded life, and a legacy of having lived in solitary confinement when the doors were wide open to so, so much more.

There also is what could be called ***identity survival***. Here, the great goal in life is to keep our projected image untarnished and to prevent others from ever doubting our competency. It is an existence unwittingly addicted to the approval of others, and chained to the opinions of fickle humans. The problem with it, among many, is that it robs us of ever truly being ourselves, and thus silences the unique shout we have to offer this world. Susan B. Anthony, a truly great radical and reformer of this country's history, put it well, *"Cautious, careful people, always casting about to preserve their reputations... can never effect a reform."* How true these words are from the leading spokesperson for the 19th century women's suffrage movement.

It strikes me that her words are a great description of identity survival — *"cautious, careful...always casting about to preserve their reputations."* When preservation of reputation becomes our highest aspiration in life, we inevitably forfeit the opportunity to leave our unique fingerprints on this world. The reason is very simple. We simply cannot show our deepest, most authentic colors without at least some criticism. And the brighter the colors, the harsher the criticism. But is it not worth it? Who wants it said at her funeral, "This person never offended anyone with her originality. She never rocked the boat. Everyone liked her, she was always so agreeable"?

This is no small issue. Do we really want our life to be summarized as, "He/she lived a risk-free, relatively comfortable existence which will be completely forgotten within the next fifty years." I think not. But that is the legacy of the vanilla-flavored life. No risk, no danger, no setbacks, no bruises…and no remembrance. This is what I call a cotton-candy life. It is a short sweet taste which has absolutely nothing to show for it at the end.

Yuck! Let me say it again — yuck and double yuck. Can that kind of milk-toast existence even remotely be considered living? Do we really want to spend our days pursuing the vanilla dream — a no dare, no criticism, no adventure life? I think not. No, I *know* not.

One of the greatest problems with choosing survival as the highest goal is that it reduces living, breathing human beings to an animal state. In the animal kingdom, survival is the great, consuming pursuit of all. No animal can write a new book, discover a new planet, find a new cure, or produce a new movie. Only man has been given the abilities for such creativity; only man can truly have dominion over the earth. How tragic to forfeit our unique opportunities as a human being by settling for that goal which defines the animal kingdom. Surely we are made for greater things than this!

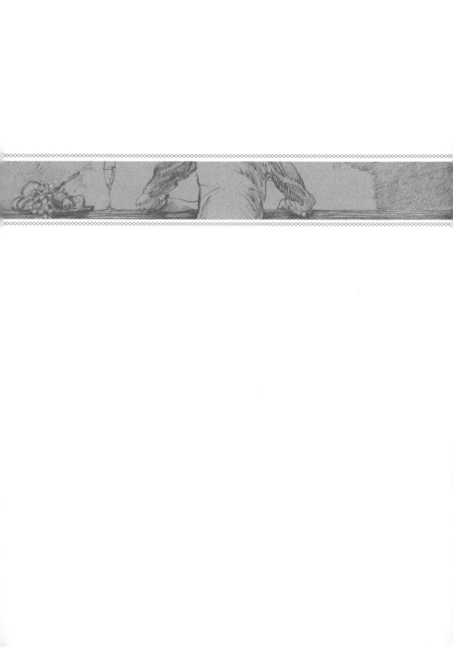

CHAPTER III The Cruise Ship — a life of tragic misappropriation

> *"He who dies with the most toys, wins."*
> **– Anonymous**

Those aboard a cruise ship have a very different agenda than those on the sinking ship. Their great goal is not *survival,* but *enjoyment.* The ship and all that it offers is there for the unbridled pleasure of the passenger.

The old beer commercial summarizes well the philosophy of so many, *"You only go around once in life, so grab all the gusto you can."* Actually I believe that statement, depending on interpretation, is right on the money. The great issue, however, is how one defines "gusto."

For those living life as though it were a cruise ship, gusto is defined in terms of wealth, prestige, dream vacations, second homes, sexual pleasures, early retirement, etc. Or perhaps it's simply a second car, a nice home, above-average income, and a growing retirement account. Not that there is anything wrong with any of these, in and of themselves. *The problem arises when legitimate pleasures become viewed as the best life has to offer.* Or, when we are seduced into believing that the wholesale enjoyment of a certain pleasure will insulate us from the pain and difficulties in the rest of our life. And most of all, when these pleasures are gripped so tightly that there is no room left in our hands for their better counterpart.

This happens when the joyous passion of unrestrained creativity is exchanged for the mere contentment of a safeguarded reputation. Or when the deep gladness of speaking kindly and powerfully into another's heart is bypassed for the temporary rest of avoided involvement. And still yet when the fiery aliveness of giving oneself unreservedly to a noble cause is relinquished for the chemically induced aliveness of excess alcohol or other drugs. Again, the problem is not with reputation, rest from involvement, or alcohol. The problem is what I like to call "an unrecognized downgrade."

If you were flying in business class and the plane attendant invited you to move up to first class, how would you respond? Almost certainly you would pick up your things and move forward, grateful for the upgrade. But suppose you were sitting in first class and the same person invited you to move back to the business section. How would you respond then? Probably not well, for no one gets excited over a downgrade; at least, not one that is recognized. And until people discern for themselves that the direction they are heading is actually a downgrade, they will not change course. It is not enough for an individual to see that the path he is taking is **wrong**. He must also see that it is **foolish** because of the potentially better path it is depriving him of.

The tragedy of living life as a cruise ship is that the passengers believe they are traveling first class when actually they have taken an unrecognized downgrade. They have settled for vanilla when they think they are having cookies and cream, chocolate chip cookie dough (my favorite), or whatever. And until they become convinced that this approach to life is actually a downgrade, they will never jump ship to get on board the actual best. I love the way Leonardo da Vinci worded it, *"He who is bound to a star turns not back."* Until we have found a more compelling star to follow, we will be prone to chase after lesser lights.

It seems to me that there are three primary objects that those aboard the cruise ship are in hot pursuit after. Each of these is derived from something good, but each has degenerated through misuse. And each is failing to deliver what it seems to be promising. In no particular order they are hedonism, materialism, and egotism.

Hedonism

This is the belief that the best life has to offer is the extreme stimulating of nerve endings. The French philosopher Voltaire epitomizes this way of thinking, *"Pleasure is the object, duty, and goal of all rational creatures."* The problem, as Voltaire's life well attests to, is that this is taking a wonderful *part* of life — the enjoyment of pleasure — and mistaking it for life itself. It is approaching a chapter in the book as though it were the whole book.

This is not to downplay the significance of pleasure in our lives. Whether it be the delight of lovemaking, the enjoyment of food and drink, the beauty of a sunset, or the smell of mountain air, all have a very important and legitimate role in our humanity. To deny them is to become subhuman. To fail to fully and properly enjoy them is to become foolish.

But to enthrone the enjoyment of pleasure as the chief end of man is to become enslaved — enslaved to appetites that can never be lastingly satisfied, chained to desires that continually ask for greater stimulation. Passengers aboard the cruise ship of hedonism are tragically adrift in a sea of discontent and futility.

Discontent, because enough is never enough when it comes to finding life through pleasure bombardment. No high is high enough, no thrill thrilling enough, no sexual encounter stimulating enough to bring to a halt the yearning for even greater pleasure encounters. As Aesop wrote, 620–560 BC, "*It is with our passions as it is with fire and water; they are good servants, but bad masters.*"

Futility, because this is the lasting legacy of a life dedicated to pleasure saturation. One's days upon this earth are never spent, they are always exchanged. Exchanged for something — meaningful or meaningless, purposeful or purposeless, lasting or fleeting. One of the great tragedies of living preeminently for pleasure is that its significance exchange rate is so desperately low:

Precious, irretrievable hours exchanged for a few laughs, some fleeting thrills, a temporary high, but no lasting influence for good. Lord Byron, the famous and extraordinarily gifted English poet spent much of his short life (died at 36) in the hot pursuit of hedonistic pleasure. On January 21, 1821, the day before his 33rd birthday, Byron wrote in his diary:

"Through life's road, so dim and dirty,
I have dragg'd to three and thirty.
What have these years left to me?
Nothing — except, thirty-three."

Does anyone really want the central theme of their funeral to be, "He or she grabbed all the pleasure they possibly could out of life. They sure had fun while it lasted"? In spite of the protest some might make, I seriously doubt if that would satisfy anyone deep down.

Somerset Maugham in his book, *Of Human Bondage*, wrote about some elderly men and women. He summarizes the tragedy of their misspent days with these words — *"These old folk had done nothing, and when they died it would be as if they had never lived."* I can hardly think of an epitaph sadder than that. For there to be no lasting footprints whatsoever from the years we crisscrossed this earth is a tragedy of monumental proportions. Yet, if no adjustment is made, essentially this will be the legacy of every passenger aboard the cruise ship "Hedonism."

Materialism

This is the belief that the best life has to offer is found in the ownership of a lot of stuff. Sounds very unsophisticated and simplistic when put like this, doesn't it? But there's a reason for stating it the way I have. Whether it be hard cash, stock certificates, 24-carat diamonds, million-dollar homes, Rolex watches, Gucci handbags, Armani suits, Rolls Royces, or everyday Wal-Mart specials; it's all just stuff. It was stuff a hundred years ago, it will be stuff a hundred years from now; and yes — like it or not — it is stuff today. Not that there is anything inherently wrong with it. Nor is there anything wrong with working diligently towards acquiring these things.

The trouble comes when good and legitimate stuff becomes North on a person's compass, and they begin to look at all of life through two lenses — *more* and *better*. More money, better house...more savings, better portfolio...more shoes, better suit...more sports equipment, better car...on and on it goes. And the great tragedy of charting this course is not the life that is spent in the pursuit of these things, but the potential life that is squandered as a result of this green-eyed hunt.

The dogged pursuit of material wealth normally has its roots in one of three motivations — status, security, or enjoyment. For some, the most important thing about wealth and material possessions is what it does for their status in society. For others, it is their source of security for whatever the future may hold. And for yet others, it is simply the sheer enjoyment of having and using nice things.

Let me say again that the problem is never with money or material things themselves. Nor is it with having and enjoying good things. All of these are a legitimate and potentially healthy part of a full-out life. The issue is the unrealistic expectations people have concerning what money and things will do for them. And the elusive chase it sends them on.

Two things always militate against materialism being the best ship to spend one's days aboard. The first, as with hedonism, is that enough is never enough. As King Solomon, one of the wisest of all men noted, *"He who loves silver will not be satisfied with silver; nor he who loves abundance, with increase."* He then goes on to note that human nature is such that whenever there is a gain in wealth there is also a commensurate gain in appetite for wealth. This is why one can never win at life through materialism, for wealth acquired always results in a new level of wealth desired. John Rockefeller was once asked how much money it took to make a man happy. His immediate and perceptive answer — "A little more." If anyone understood this from experience, surely it was he. It has been my experience that the only genuinely content wealthy men and women I know have always found their contentment outside of wealth, never through it.

Secondly, all the wealth one acquires on this earth is immediately forfeited at the instant of death. Following the funeral of a very wealthy man, one of his friends said to another, "Just how much do you think John left behind?" The friend rightly responded, "Everything."

Just as when a game of Monopoly is over and everyone returns their make-believe assets to be put away, so is the day of one's departure from this earth. Everything, but everything a man or woman has stored up is instantly passed over to others for safekeeping and enjoyment. Nothing…please hear me well…nothing we have managed to acquire on this earth departs with us on our death. The Spanish proverb says it well, "*There are no pockets in the shroud.*" Another quips, "*You have never seen a U-Haul on the back of a hearse.*"

Though one cannot take anything with them, this does not negate the importance of diligence, hard work, and the sweat-soaked pursuit of a better kind of life. Laziness is not the antidote to materialism. But the problem arises when quantity of possessions is equated with quality of life. Or when one begins to believe that owning the newest and the nicest is the best life has to offer. And especially, when significance of life is aborted at the hands of the grasping for more stuff. William James, pioneering American psychologist, was exactly right, "*The greatest use of life is to spend it for something that will outlast it.*"

Egotism

This is the belief that the best life has to offer is found in being respected by others and adored by self. It is malignant self-confidence. And it is the single most odious trait any man or woman can possess, though its stench is rarely recognized by the infected person.

As with both hedonism and materialism, egotism is the mismanagement of something inherently good. It is taking the normal and natural need for a healthy self-image, and grotesquely twisting it out of proportion. Thinking positively about oneself is transformed into worshipping oneself; and all of life is now expected to follow suit.

The danger of choosing egotism (which is usually an unrecognized choice) is threefold. First, it robs us of the single most important virtue in life — humility. This character trait, in my opinion, is the soil from which everything great in a man or woman's life grows. As English poet and philosopher John Ruskin taught, "*I believe the first test of a truly great man is his humility. I do not mean by humility doubt of his own power or hesitation in speaking his opinion. But really great men have a feeling…that the greatness is not in them but through them…*"

Secondly, egotism can never be fully satisfied. As with hedonism and materialism, enough is never enough. No amount of praise can eradicate the desire for more praise, no award can override the longing for more and greater awards, no headline can lastingly quell the yearning for even greater headlines.

Thirdly, those who scratch and claw to insure that their name be remembered are very often forgotten. Or if they are remembered, it is often negatively. Ironically it is those who have lived life radically for a noble cause, with little or no regard for their own reputation, who most often are the highly revered among men. "*How some men struggle into obscurity, while others forget themselves into immortality,*" wrote Phillips Brooks, noted American clergyman and author. Cecil Rhodes left England to amass a huge fortune through diamond mining in South Africa. Along the way, he insured that his name would be remembered through the establishment of a well-endowed fund for promising scholars — known today as the Rhodes Scholarship. He also managed to get a country named after himself; Rhodesia. Ironically, one of the last things he said on his deathbed was this, *"Well, at least they can't change the name of a country, can they?"* But they did, didn't they. Rhodesia is now replaced by Zimbabwe.

Look at those who are remembered most favorably throughout the history of mankind. Are they not the ones who "forgot themselves into immortality"? Mother Teresa, Gandhi, Lincoln, Martin Luther King, and the greatest of all for my money — Jesus of Nazareth.

The tragedy of the cruise-ship approach to life is that irretrievable opportunities for mighty and significant living are forever forfeited in exchange for mere cotton candy. After all, that's really what hedonism, materialism, and egotism are in the final analysis: A short, sweet taste which can never deeply satisfy the soul nor carve out a lasting mark of influence. And a cotton-candy life makes a cotton-candy difference in this world, leaving a cotton-candy legacy in its wake.

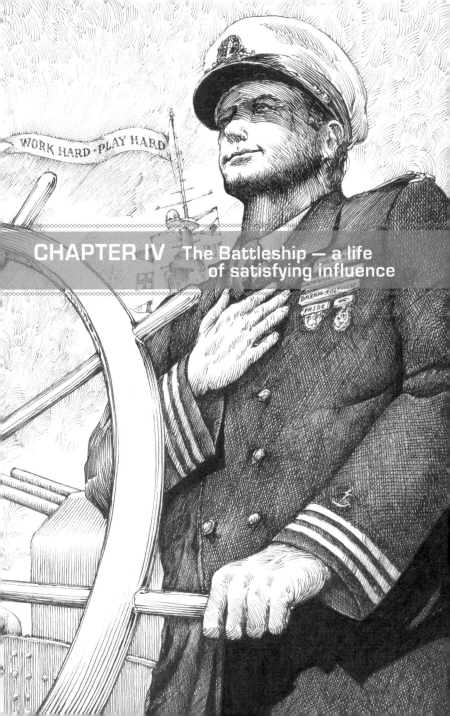

WORK HARD · PLAY HARD

CHAPTER IV The Battleship — a life of satisfying influence

> *"Many persons have a wrong idea of what constitutes true happiness. It is not attained through self-gratification but through fidelity to a worthy purpose."*
>
> **– Helen Keller**

Those aboard a battleship have a far greater (and certainly more adventurous) purpose than those aboard the previous two ships. Those on the battleship are there to make a difference, to fight for a cause, to have significant impact. And that's how I would describe the lives of those choosing this third and final ship. Their great goal in life is not merely **survival** or **enjoyment**, but **influence**. Influence that makes a difference on others, influence that arises from the deepest parts within them, influence that has their unique fingerprints all over it, influence that shouts to the world — "It *mattered* that I lived!" penned playwright George Bernard Shaw,

"*This is the true joy in life, the being used for a purpose recognized by yourself as a mighty one: the being thoroughly worn out before you are thrown on the scrap heap, and being a force of nature instead of a feverish, selfish little clod of ailments and grievances complaining that the world will not devote itself to making you happy."*

This influence, it seems to me, has two central components. First, it is an influence that centers upon what I like to term "a noble cause." Influence can be a wonderful or awful commodity, depending upon the form it takes. Consider the following contrasts:

Plato and Nero
Lincoln and Hitler
Gandhi and Stalin
Florence Nightingale and Marie Antoinette

I'm sure you get the point. Every good thing has the potential for abuse. A scalpel can be used for healing or mutilation; dynamite can help build highways or destroy people. Influence is exactly the same. It can be used for great good and equally great harm. But the kind of influence I am talking about is that which ennobles and benefits us, the people around us, and society at large. It is the kind of influence that one has no regrets taking to the grave.

This is why I like to call it a "noble cause." This cause will vary from individual to individual. Its size and scope may be large or small. But whatever it is, it will always lead to an upgrade of existence for those around. If it doesn't, better to stay on one of the first two ships.

The second characteristic of this influence is that it is uniquely fitted to the individual. It is what I like to term a person's "extraordinary dream." Not everyone can sing a great song, write a best-selling novel, discover a needed cure, or create a new invention. But everyone can do what they are uniquely wired and gifted for. And it is that potential which makes it possible for every person's life to be extraordinary, whether the world takes notice of it or not. As famed Austrian psychiatrist and Holocaust survivor Viktor Frankl said, *"Everyone has his own specific vocation or mission in life; everyone must carry out a concrete assignment that demands fulfillment. Therein he cannot be replaced, nor can his life be repeated, thus, everyone's task is unique as his specific opportunity."*

Again, let me say as clearly and loudly as I know how, extraordinary does not mean clearly visible or publicly sensational. Most people's extraordinary dream is lived out in the shadows, away from the public view. It is the single mother who raises her children as best she possibly can, often with little or no help. It is the postal worker who recognizes the nobility of his task and plays it to the hilt. It is the elementary school teacher, grossly underpaid for the monumental contribution she is making to society for the influencing of future leaders. A dream need not be publicly grandiose to be extraordinary. It only need be uniquely fitted to the individual.

Beyond this, it is only in the pursuit and unfolding of an extraordinary dream that any individual will be most energized and fulfilled. Until we are operating out of the center of our giftedness, our soul will never know that wonderful paradox of being enflamed and at rest simultaneously. American psychologist and author Abraham Maslow observed, "*...a new discontent and restlessness will soon develop unless the individual is doing what he is fitted for. A musician must make music, an artist must paint, a poet must write, if he is to be ultimately happy. What a man can be, he must be.*"

Let those words sink down deeply into your being. There is a song only *you* can sing, a work only *you* can perform, a gap only *you* can fill, a part made only for *you* and *you* for it. And that is your extraordinary dream, your monogrammed vision beckoning you to life extraordinaire. This is exactly what painter and sculptor Pablo Picasso was getting at when he wrote, "*It is your work in life that is the ultimate seduction.*" In other words, passionately embracing your unique calling in life will bring greater and deeper soul satisfaction than any allurement this world has to offer.

I like to call this "hearing the click of the shotgun." This comes from observing the dog of a friend of mine, a dog who must be a zillion years old. The poor thing is riddled with arthritis, and it is just flat painful to watch him inch his way to his food bowl and back. But when my friend goes to his gun cabinet, pulls down his shotgun, and the dog hears the click of the shotgun; something just amazing begins to transpire. His ears go up, his tail begins to wag, new light comes into his eyes, and he begins to move far more quickly. And guess what? My friend still takes him hunting, and while he is out running after the prey, you would never know that anything is wrong. But once he comes home, and the guns are put away, he returns to his pitiful self.

Why this transformation? Very simple. My friend's dog is a hunting dog. He was made by God to hunt and run down prey. No one taught him that this is what he should do; it is simply his inbred instinct. Nothing makes him more alive or energizes him more fully than the thrill of the hunt. If he were a herding dog, the click of the shotgun would mean nothing to him.

May I ask you a question my dear reader? Have you heard the click of the shotgun? For you? Have you found that which energizes and excites your inner being like nothing else? That talent or gift or purpose which launches you out into the world with greater passion than anything else? It's there; just don't give up on finding it. For me personally, it is speaking and writing. Growing up this wasn't something I aspired to in any shape or form. But over the years I've come to discover an undeniable reality. Nothing more passionately energizes or deeply satisfies me than communicating what I perceive to be important truth in hopefully vivid and memorable ways. Whether it be through writing or speaking, there is a high I find in communicating that outstrips anything else I try to do. And there is an unsought depth of satisfaction that comes with this same territory. As best I can tell, this is what God wired me to do above all else. For me, it is my "click of the shotgun."

How then does one go about finding their unique calling and extraordinary dream? Their click of the shotgun? The answer to this question is not easy, and it certainly isn't mechanical or formulaic. The way it comes varies from individual to individual, and therefore defies any single, cookie cutter, one-size-fits-all answer.

Here are some guidelines which I believe can help you in finding your dream. Or, more often than not, your dream finding you.

Seek to discover your dream, not create it. There must be a relaxed pursuit in finding one's extraordinary dream. As I previously alluded to, this dream will most likely find you before you find it. What I mean is that it will have been quietly and patiently preparing the soil of your heart long before its vision is ever planted in your mind. And when the dream hits you, it will not feel so much like you have found something new as that you have genuinely come home at last.

Joan is a stay-at-home mom with three children under six. Most days, survival is her primary goal, and understandably so. But something had been stirring in her and that just wouldn't leave her alone. It was the vision of seeing her and other mothers with young children coming together one night a month to discuss a mutually agreed upon book and share their struggles and joys of motherhood. This dream, in her words, "kept hunting her down."

Finally she gave in, asked some other mothers what they thought about meeting together, and the first group was quickly born. Soon other groups, like theirs, began springing up. Now dozens of young mothers are tremendously benefitting each month from the dream that Joan could not shake. And, as she told me, "It just feels like this is what I was made for!" She had discovered her extraordinary dream rather than trying to create one.

When you find your dream there will be an intangible but very real sense of "*This* is where I belong, *this* is what I was made for, *this* is where I feel most centered." Aleksandr Solzhenitsyn, a novelist, dramatist and historian, said as a young man, "*I knew I was born to write.*"

That's not to say that this feeling of centeredness won't be accompanied by a sense of trepidation, insecurity, maybe even terror at the prospect of what now lies ahead. But even these things cannot prevent the soul from recognizing and enjoying its homecoming.

It is absolutely imperative, therefore, that you not rush this dream. Pursue finding it — yes. But in the pursuit beware of the temptation to speed things up by subtly (and usually unconsciously) creating a dream of one's own making. Too many people have settled for a second-tier dream of their own invention and thereby missed the first-tier one they were made for. And second-tier dreams can never bring first-tier satisfaction or influence.

A good way to begin finding your first-tier dream is to ponder how you would answer the following questions:

1. What would you most like to do if money were not an issue?
2. What would you most like to do if family responsibilities were not an issue?
3. What would you most like to do if geographical location was not an issue?

4. What most easily energizes and excites you? What topic of conversation brings new light to your eyes?
5. What non-required topic(s) do you find yourself most often reading about?
6. What work, though still tiring, leaves you energized rather than drained?
7. What quietly nags at you from within during times of reflection upon your life?
8. If you had to get a graduate degree, what would you most enjoy studying?
9. What are you truly afraid to admit that you would most enjoy accomplishing?

The answers to these questions should help to narrow the leading candidates for your extraordinary dream.

An important influence is the people you spend time with. American essayist, philosopher and poet, Ralph Waldo Emerson said, *"Show me with whom you are found, and I will tell you who you are."*

When I give talks to incoming college freshmen, I will normally ask them what they think the most important decision they will ever make in college is. Usually I get answers like "choosing my major" or "how I spend my free time." Then I tell them what I believe it to be: who you choose as your closest friends. Nothing more profoundly affects a student's years in college than the peer group he or she chooses to run with. I've yet to find a teacher, administrator or coach to disagree with that.

Those with dreams should *"surround themself with*

Reprinted with permission of the McGraw-Hill Companies from *The Leadership Secrets of Colin Powell* by Oren Harari © 2002.

people who take their work seriously, but not themselves; people who work hard and play hard," explains Colin Powell, American statesman and former four-star general. We all need the heat of others to rekindle our flickering flame for significant living.

J. R. R. Tolkien, C. S. Lewis, George MacDonald, Owen Barfield and several other outstanding British writers were members of a group named The Inklings. These writers met once a week to critique each other's writings, chat about various topics and simply enjoy one another's company. Each of them credits that group and their times together as a very significant contributing factor to their success.

Take inventory of your gifts, talents, and desires. Whatever your extraordinary dream is, it will fit you and you will fit it. Fulfilling it will undoubtedly require much hard work and relentless perseverance. But when an extraordinary dream matches your giftedness, its required work energizes you more than it drains you. And you find a joyous fulfillment in that task which keeps you from wandering in search of something else. This is what author and business speaker Harvey Mackay was alluding to when he wrote, *"Find something you love to do and you'll never have to work a day in your life."*

This is where you might seriously consider taking some of the tests on the market for aptitudes, temperaments, and vocations. Just out of curiosity, I took one recently and was amazed how accurately it described me, my abilities, and what vocations I would be good at. None of these tests are infallible, nor do they perfectly gauge any person. But they can be very helpful in narrowing the field of possibilities so one has a clearer focus on what to be considering.

Another important step in this is to ask individuals who know you well (parents, teachers, and trusted friends) what things they notice you do especially well, and what things appear to most fulfill you. Oftentimes others can see our unique giftedness before we can.

Try to touch bottom as to what you would most like to do. What I mean by this is that it can be very, very difficult to get down to the depths in our being where our most vital dream lies. It is much like swimming and trying to touch bottom in very deep water. You're not sure how far down the bottom is, so you swim down to see if you can touch it. But often there comes a point where you haven't hit bottom yet and you're afraid to go down any further, so you shoot back up to the top.

I really believe that this is true of many people in their pilgrimage through life. Too few of us have the courage to go down deep enough to look our most important dream in the eye, call it by name, and bring it up to the surface. It requires tremendous courage to make it that far. Julia Cameron, teacher, artist, poet, and filmmaker, observes, "*Each of us has an inner dream that we can unfold if we will just have the courage to admit what it is. And the faith to trust our own admission. The admitting is often very difficult.*"

What things keep us from touching bottom in finding our dream? We have already mentioned courage, which is a huge one. Another is the fear of it being impractical. For one to find their extraordinary dream, the issue of practicality must be temporarily set aside. Of course it seems impractical, of course it's hard to see how it could ever work out, of course others will scorn it as being unrealistic, otherwise, it wouldn't be a dream big enough to be worth your while. As Albert Einstein said, *"If at first, the idea is not absurd, then there is no hope for it."*

There were hundreds of reasons why the commercially feasible lightbulb should never have been invented, but none powerful enough to stop Thomas Alva Edison from carrying out his extraordinary dream.

Another huge detriment to finding one's dream is the fear of what others will think, especially loved ones. It is very difficult to hear the beckoning of one's dream while worrying over how others will respond to it. Fear of criticism has a paralyzing effect on being able to reach out and take hold of the dream we were made for. Swiss physician and psychologist Paul Tournier put it well, *"…in all fields, even those of culture and art, other people's judgment exercises a paralyzing effect. Fear of criticism kills spontaneity; it prevents men from showing themselves and expressing themselves freely, as they are. Much courage is needed to paint a picture, to write a book, to erect a building designed along new architectural lines, or to formulate an independent opinion or an original idea."*

Finally there is fear of the unknown. How will it all turn out? What are the specific steps that we must take in order to achieve our extraordinary dream? What can we absolutely count on? These are the security-driven questions which we all would like answered up front.

Problem is — our extraordinary dream rarely, if ever, comes with prepackaged instructions. The answers come only after we have launched out into the risky and adventurous waters of personal dream-seizing. But out there the seas are uncharted, the weather unpredictable, and the waves often threaten to capsize our ship. Fear of the unknown has kept many a life safely in the harbor, anchored securely to a totally predictable and manageable existence. But it has also separated them from the kind of excitement and wide-eyed adventure that all of our souls long for. And one's existence can easily become that described by J. R. R. Tolkien in *The Hobbit* when Bilbo first meets Gandalf, "*We are a plain, quiet folk and have no use for adventures.*" Surely life was never meant to be that boringly routine or excitement-starved.

Pray. This is not my attempt to get churchy, preachy, or religious on you. But I cannot write about this aspect of our lives without relating it to what I believe to be the Center of our existence. My first two books (*Revolution Within* and *Releasing the Rivers Within*) lay out my understanding of true spirituality versus tired and rigid religiosity. In them I seek to demonstrate that man is a created being with a delegated purpose in life. This delegated purpose (i.e. one's extraordinary dream) is determined and designed by God. Therefore, one of the most important pursuits in finding one's extraordinary dream should be an upward, dependent one. And this is where prayer enters in.

Be open to a dream that could totally disrupt

your life. This is very likely the most difficult part of the whole equation. An extraordinary dream almost always comes at an extraordinary price. To resolutely take hold of what you were made for may well turn your world upside-down, and possibly that of others around you. And therein lays one of the greatest difficulties — the impact our dream might have on others' lives.

A friend told me about a dream he has and then followed it up with, "If only I didn't have a wife and kids, I would go for it right now." That's very understandable, and he is to be commended for his sense of responsibility. But I just wonder if he won't become another in the long line of individuals who assume their dream will cost others so much that it isn't worth the pursuit. And then the dream is put to bed in the dormitory of the soul, never to disturb anyone else — but never to excite, enflame, or energize the person with a reason for living that outstrips anything he or she has ever known before. Though they may seek to find a substitute lifework, none can resonate as deeply or passionately as the one they have said "good night" to.

Also, you can't know the potential good your dream might bring to others as well. As I told my friend, "But what a great gift you would be giving them — a husband and father fully alive, more centered than ever, and daily demonstrating the courage and persistence of pursuing an extraordinary dream. Isn't this what you want your children to do? The most influential thing you can do, then, is model it." We'll see what happens, but all indications are that he is in the process of grabbing hold of his dream.

There is a wide variety of disruptions your dream may bring. Often it is vocational disruption — leaving a secure, comfortable job for the unrealized promise of what could be. This is exactly what John Sculley did in 1983 when he left a very prestigious position at Pepsico to become president of a young, upstart company called Apple Computers. What caused him to take the risk? It was a question Steve Jobs, cofounder of Apple, goaded him with: *Do you want to spend the rest of your life selling sugar water, or do you want to help change the world?* He took the dare to be a world-changer and followed his extraordinary dream.

There are very often relational disruptions. Parents and spouses can very often be unenthused, to put it mildly, by your new vision and direction. There can be geographical disruption — often pulling up stakes which are deeply and securely driven, to move to a brand-new location with brand-new people and to start brand-new all over again. Not many people get excited about that. Yet our country was fundamentally settled by those kinds of risk-takers. Or financial disruption: having to live on a substantially diminished budget in order to pursue your extraordinary dream. Dream-chasing is an immensely impractical issue with immensely impractical costs. If you don't think that's true, it may be because you've never tried it.

There is no shortage of reasons why you shouldn't pursue your extraordinary dream. There normally is no lack of people to tell you why the dream can't work. Why you should stop chasing the wind and get on with real life in the real world. As French philosopher and mathematician Blaise Pascal wrote, *"The highest order of mind is accused of folly, as well as the lowest. Nothing is thoroughly approved but mediocrity. The majority has established this, and fixes its fangs on whatever gets beyond it either way."*

All these hindrances can become very convincing. But none of them can fully still the internal restlessness of a dream put on hold. None of them can offer a replacement for the joyous passion of daring to dream the extraordinary dream. And none of them can provide that whisper in your inner ear, echoing forth from profoundly satisfied parts deep within, *"This* is why you were born."

It is only the battleship crew who know whereof I speak — those men and women captivated by a life-transforming vision of what could be, enflamed by possibilities temporarily out of grasp, and energized to attack their dream with unreserved diligence and relentless perseverance. They refuse to merely exist in the valley of rote responsibility, but rather to soar to the fresh, unexplored heights of actualizing their extraordinary dream. They and they alone understand what Thoreau was talking about when he wrote, *"Our truest life is when we are in dreams awake."* When it is all said and done, it is only the pursuit of an extraordinary dream which infuses men and women with extraordinary vitality and an extraordinary purpose for living.

But let it be said again, the pursuit of an extraordinary dream is no walk in the park. Viral insights and significant discoveries of truth never come quickly, easily or free-of-charge. They are brought forth through sweat, effort and long periods of time. And very often, it is not the smartest, the cleverest, or the most imaginative person who brings home the bacon at the end of the day. It is the most doggedly persevered. This is exactly what physicist Albert Einstein was referring to when he said, *"It's not that I'm so smart, it's just that I stay with the problem longer."*

Edison shared that belief. He performed over 10,000 experiments before discovering the right filament for the lightbulb. His assistant, at one point, said in exasperation, "We have tried thousands of experiments, and they all failed. We've had no results whatsoever," To which Edison replied, "Results? Why, man, I have gotten lots of results! If I find 10,000 ways something won't work, I haven't failed."

Something else about Edison required him to have much courage and perseverance — he had a handicap. He didn't talk until he was four. At age seven, his teacher considered him "addled" or confused and not teachable, and his father concurred. His mother began to educate him. By twelve, his hearing had deteriorated until he became 100 percent deaf in his left ear and 80 percent in his right ear.

However, what Edison had going for him in spades was an insatiable hunger to learn, a remarkable ability to work, and a relentless, never say die commitment to persevere. His inventions revolutionized modern society. He was responsible for the photograph, the stock ticker, the movie camera, and for making the lightbulb commercially feasible, plus hundreds of other inventions and 1,093 U.S. patents. *Life* magazine placed him first on a list of the "100 Most Important People in the Last 1,000 Years."

Edison was not the only person who did not let a handicap hold him back. Michael Guido, columnist, observed: *"A sound body, a brilliant mind, a cultural background, a huge amount of money, a wonderful education — none of these guarantee success. Booker T. Washington was born in slavery. Thomas Edison was deaf. Abraham Lincoln was born of illiterate parents. Lord Byron had a clubfoot. Robert Louis Stevenson had tuberculosis. Alexander Pope was a hunchback. Admiral Horatio Nelson had only one eye. Julius Caesar was an epileptic. Louis Pasteur was nearsighted and Helen Keller, who could not hear or see, graduated from college with honors."*

In 1962, Victor and Mildred Goertzel published a fascinating study, "Cradles of Eminence," of 413 famous and exceptionally gifted people focusing on the most common reasons for success. The single most common denominator in each of these lives was that almost each of them had to overcome very difficult obstacles in order to become who they were.

"Whatever you do, you need courage. Whatever course you decide upon, there is always someone to tell you that you are wrong. There are always difficulties arising that tempt you to believe your critics are right. To map out a course of action and follow it to an end requires some of the same courage that a soldier needs," wrote Emerson.

The importance of perseverance can hardly be overstated. One of its most significant contributions to the seizing of our extraordinary dream is its ability to doggedly exhaust all possibilities of thought concerning the dream. This requires at least two fundamental, underlying beliefs. Without them it will be very difficult to sustain the mental endurance necessary to take our thinking to the highest summit. And almost always it takes this kind of creative tenacity to find the blueprints for an extraordinary dream.

The first is the realization that great possibilities for advancement are frequently dismissed solely because they also have great possibilities for abuse. This is often referred to as "slippery slope logic." Ideas are rejected solely because they might head in a bad or unhelpful direction. Yet this, it seems to me, is one of the absolutely weakest reasons for idea dismissal. Almost everything that can bring great benefit can also bring great harm. Dynamite was originally invented with the intent of helping mankind in construction and tunnel-building. In a very short period it was also being used for destruction of mankind. Vaccines were initially opposed. British physician Edward Jenner was sneered at for developing a small pox vaccine using cow pox. It was reported that, "Some serious minded men said that all animal diseases would be transferred to the human race. Some said they had actually seen horns growing out of the foreheads of innocent people." But can you imagine where we would be today without them?

Outside-the-box thinking is never done well by

vanilla lovers, those easily gratified souls who are quietly satisfied with conventional thinking. They possess no desire to venture out into the potential storms of perspective upheaval. It is only the true pioneers who walk boldly toward the storms, not because they love the conflict but because they relish the opportunity to grab hold of the lightning bolts of fresh and innovative thinking. And they will not be dissuaded by the guise of potential abuse.

The second critical belief concerning perseverance is that exhausting creativity and mind-numbing searching *will* pay off. This is no easy certainty to come by. All too often we quit paying the price that seizing the best requires because we lose heart that diligence will ever win the day. Thomas Edison was right, *"Many of life's failures are people who did not realize how close they were to success when they gave up."* Einstein wrote, *"I think and think for months and years. Ninety-nine times, the conclusion is false. The hundredth time I am right."* What the world owes to those brave and persistent souls who refused to go quietly and timidly into the night with their extraordinary dreams! Einstein, for instance, could have contented himself with teaching a little high school math, puttering around in his garden, playing cards with his friends, and finding a hobby or two to fill up whatever time he had left over. Can you imagine the tragic difference that would have meant to the world?

How then can we go about developing and sustaining this vital ability to persevere at all costs? While there are several things that are important, one towers above all the rest in my thinking — Perspective. Simply put, where we focus our eyes profoundly determines the way in which we live our lives. And the way in which we place one faltering step in front of another until our dream has been finally hunted down. Let me suggest three critical thoughts concerning perspective and its impact on perseverance.

Exploit the Power of Perspective. I very purposefully use the word "exploit" here. It is one thing to utilize something; it is a very different thing to exploit it. What I mean is to drain every possible ounce of benefit from it. To drink it dry, to seize its every advantage, to utterly maximize its possibilities. Most people are aware of the power of perspective; only vanilla-busters master the fine art of exploiting that power. There is so, so much power in gaining and maintaining the right perspective. Proper perspective does not just happen. It must be fought for, clung to…and exploited for all it is worth.

Nothing is more crucial to perseverance than perspective. How we view the obstacles, challenges and difficulties facing us will profoundly determine the ways in which we respond to them. Stephen Covey, author, is right when he says, *"Our problem is the way we see our problem."* Without exception I can say that the greatest failures in my life all began with a blurred perspective on the matter at hand. And, whatever successes there have been were profoundly determined by the point of view I approached them from as well.

Our ability to persevere in the present is largely determined by our ability to focus on the future. It is much like what happened to Florence Chadwick, the first woman to swim the English Channel in both directions.

On July 4, 1951, she stepped out into the Pacific in an attempt to swim from Catalina Island to the California coast. The challenge was not just the distance but also the bone-chilling waters of the Pacific. To complicate matters, a dense fog lay over the entire area, making it impossible for her to see land. After 15 hours in the water and within a half-mile of her goal, Chadwick gave up. Just as she was pulled into the boat, the fog lifted and she could see the shoreline. Later she told a reporter, *"Look, I'm not excusing myself, but if I could have seen land, I might have made it."*

Not long afterward she attempted the feat again. Once more a misty veil obscured the coastline. But this time she kept reminding herself of the shore that was there. Buoyed by that perspective, she bravely swam on and achieved her goal. In fact, she broke the men's record by two hours!

When we focus only upon the costs and sacrifices attached to our dream, we are like Florence Chadwick swimming in the fog with no sight of the land before us. But as we take time to continually remind ourselves of the shore before us (i.e. the satisfaction and reward of actualizing our extraordinary dream), our spirits are buoyed and we are enabled to continue persevering. Perspective makes all the difference!

EPILOGUE

> "*Two roads diverged in a wood, and I — I took the one less traveled by, and that has made all the difference.*"
> **– Robert Frost**

Three ships, three tales to be told, three legacies left behind. Which ship are you on right now? Have the courage to be brutally honest in answering. Which ship do you sense calling you by name, beckoning you to throw caution to the wind and come aboard unreservedly? Surely it is the battleship.

That is not to say it is wrong to ever venture upon the other ships. There are times that the sinking ship is our only choice. There will be periods in our life that survival is extraordinary living. Likewise, there are times to treat life as a cruise ship and enjoy its good gifts to the hilt. All soldiers need their times of rest and recreation. The great issue is which ship we make *primary* in our lives.

Only those who choose this third ship know what it is to say "no" to vanilla and "yes" to life. They are those unique individuals who refuse to settle down in the lowlands of merely surviving life or enjoying it. Instead they are resolved to scale the mountaintops of discovering their truest calling, of maximizing their fullest potential, of seizing their highest destiny, and of breathing the purest air this life has to offer.

They are the radical minority who are attacking life with well-directed and unrestrained passion, who are taking the road less traveled, who are refusing to merely exist, who will not go quietly into the night, or live dull, blunted lives. Rather, they know the high adventure, the wide-eyed drama, and the fiery exuberance of giving oneself unreservedly to a noble and uniquely fitted task.

It is desperately easy however, for our extraordinary dream to slip through our fingers. Many have begun well only to be sidelined by the cost. Sincere as we may be in seizing our highest destiny, it takes far more than good intentions for our extraordinary dream to become extraordinary reality. I close this book with five things necessary for one to grab hold of life's best. I call them "the five fingers of dream seizing."

Vision — In the hand imagery, I liken this to the thumb. It undergirds and supports the work of the other four. Vision is the ability to see and believe that what we seek to grasp is of more value and personal benefit than what we are giving up. It has often been referred to as "envisioning a preferable future." Unless we are internally convinced that what we are reaching for is preferable to what we are holding on to, there is no way we are going to risk grasping the new, especially if it is anything remotely important. Vision lays the foundation for courageous actions which are normally preceded by a renovated perspective. It is this tremendous power of vision that President Woodrow Wilson was referring to when he wrote, *"We grow great by dreams. All big men are dreamers. They see things in the soft haze of a spring day or in the red fire of a long winter's evening. Some of us let these great dreams die, but others nourish and protect them; nurse them through bad days till they bring them to the sunshine and light which comes always to those who sincerely hope that their dreams will come true."*

Only when we are able to see the situation or opportunity in a new light, only when we are able to view it in a new perspective and are captivated by the vision of what could be, will we take the risks necessary to seize the prize. Or be able to nurse our dream through good days and bad.

Risk — The second finger is risk-taking and is at the very heart of dream seizing. Only if we are willing to hazard our present security and comfort will we reach out and take hold of our extraordinary dream and seize irretrievable opportunities.

That's why it is called *taking a risk*, not *receiving a sure thing*. When we focus primarily on the risk, the crisis and the cost, it becomes easy to lose heart and return to the land of safekeeping. But when we can gaze past the danger zone to the opportunity waiting to be seized, this renewed perspective often provides the internal firepower that helps thrust us forward.

T. S. Eliot was exactly right when he wrote, *"Only those who will risk going too far can possibly find out how far one can go."* Big dreams never come to fruition through small risks. It was through big risks, frightening as they often were, that Columbus discovered the new world, the pilgrims came to America, Rosa Parks refused to give up her seat on the bus, Martin Luther King Jr. led the civil rights movement, and countless others have secured their extraordinary dream. And so it is today.

Sacrifice — The third finger of courage is sacrifice; it is usually bruised, bleeding and sometimes broken, because it is the finger which picks up the tab for the commitment made by vision and risk.

"It is only through labor and painful effort, by grim energy and resolute courage that we move onto better things," emphasized Theodore Roosevelt, who before becoming U.S. vice president then president, organized the first U.S. Volunteer Cavalry Regiment — the Rough Riders — during the Spanish-American War.

Simply put, there is no such thing as costless dream seizing. Milton rose at 4:00 a.m. every day in order to have enough hours for his *Paradise Lost*. Noah Webster labored 36 years writing his dictionary, crossing the Atlantic twice to gather material. Edward Gibbon spent 26 years on his *Decline and Fall of the Roman Empire*. William Wilberforce fought for 55 years to abolish slavery in England and the British Empire. It came as he lay on his deathbed.

Launching out in pursuit of an extraordinary dream and exchanging the safe harbor of vanilla living for the threatening seas of radical living will always incur multifaceted sacrifices along the journey.

Wisdom — The fourth finger enables you to know which risks and which opportunities are worthy candidates. Not every risk is worth taking. There is a difference between courage, recklessness, and foolhardiness. A crucial difference.

Custer's Last Stand on June 25, 1876, is an outstanding example of this. He had been ordered to await troop reinforcements, but chose to attack anyway. He knew, but knew, that he and his men were overwhelmingly outnumbered. He and his 200 soldiers perished within in a two hour battle; not because of his courage but his unchecked ego. What he displayed on that battlefield was recklessness, foolhardiness, and hubris. But certainly not wisdom. All dream seizing requires courage. But a courage that takes the right risk at the right time in the right way for the right reason. And this requires the critical commodity of wisdom.

Resolve — The final finger of the hand of dream seizing is resolve. It is the determined act of the will to mightily take hold of our preferable future. It is the resolute decision to no longer debate with ourself; to actually stretch forth the hand, and to actually put it unreservedly on the plough. Or to use another image, it is the unswerving commitment to burn our ships.

That is exactly what explorer Hernando Cortez did in 1519 after he landed on the coast of Mexico. Knowing that his men would be sorely tempted to return to the Old World prematurely, he gave orders that all the ships be burned. Setting aside for the moment the fact that greed and ego appear to be the controlling motivations behind his decision, it was a brilliant move psychologically. When all hope of retreating back to safety is gone, moving forward through the dangers is the only remaining option.

Resolve is the superglue which keeps the hand of courage from slipping off the handlebar of opportunity. Without it our best intentions remain but intentions, our loftiest dreams remain out of reach, our highest aspirations go unrealized, and our potential successes are relegated to "what might have been" status. But through it, we are enabled to decisively stay on track and reach our extraordinary dream.

It requires all five fingers for the hand of dream seizing to not slip off the bar of opportunity. Without vision, an extraordinary dream will soon lose steam and ultimately die out. Without risk, it will have no punch. It will leave no significant impact or make any radical change. Without sacrifice, it will have no buying power or enough currency to produce a difference. Its good intentions will remain but that. Without wisdom, it will have no solid directionality. Bravehearted living will be stranded without a map or compass. Without resolve, it will have no staying power.

But extraordinary dreams are seized by fingers invigorated by vision, marked by risk-taking, funded by sacrifice, directed by wisdom, and sustained by resolve. Few people have articulated the cost and glory of this kind of dream seizing better than Theodore Roosevelt when he wrote,

"*It is not the critic who counts; not the man who points*

out how the strong man stumbles, or where the doer of deeds could have done them better. The credit belongs to the man who is actually in the arena, whose face is marred by dust and sweat and blood, who strives valiantly; who errs and comes short again and again; because there is not effort without error and shortcomings; but who does actually strive to do the deed; who knows the great enthusiasm, the great devotion, who spends himself in a worthy cause, who at the best knows in the end the triumph of high achievement and who at the worst, if he fails, at least he fails while daring greatly. So that his place shall never be with those cold and timid souls who know neither victory nor defeat. Far better it is to dare mighty things, to win glorious triumphs even though checkered by failure, than to rank with those poor spirits who neither enjoy nor suffer much because they live in the gray twilight that knows neither victory nor defeat."

I urge you, my reader, say "no" to the gray twilight which knows neither victory nor defeat. Say "no" to being a cold and timid soul. Say "no" to being a sideline critic. Say "yes" to being actually in the arena, with your face marred by dust and sweat and blood. Say "yes" to knowing the great enthusiasm and the great devotion of daring to spend yourself in a worthy cause. Say "yes" to living life aboard the battleship and influencing this world through your noble and uniquely fitted dream. And when it's all said and done, may your eulogy inspire succeeding generations to give up their petty and shallow pursuits in exchange for a life that leaves mighty and lasting fingerprints on this world. *Carpe diem*…seize the day.

Endnotes

p. 12 Christopher Columbus (1451–1506), *Our Country Begins* by Philip J. Furlong, Helen M. Ganey, Francis Downing; W. H. Sadler Inc., © 1941 Edition M

p. 19 *Alfred Nobel*, A Biography by Kenne Fant, © 1991; translation © 1993 by Arcade Publishing Inc., NY

p. 21 Tim McGraw, country music artist, August 2004 album "Live Like You Were Dying" (Curb Records).

p. 21 Steve Jobs' 2005 graduation speech text at Stanford University, http://news-service.stanford.edu/news/2005/june15/jobs-061505

pp. 28 & 52 Abraham Maslow, 1908–1970, Hierarchy of Human Needs from his paper, "Theory of Human Motivation," *Psychological Review*, vol. 50, no. 4, 1943.

pp. 27, 29, 63 Henry David Thoreau, *Walden and Other Writings*, Random House, Inc., NY, © 1965, ISBN: 0-679-78334-2

p. 30 Scoutmaster Forest Whitcraft, from an essay, "Within My Power," first published in Scouting Magazine, Oct. 1950.

p. 30 *C. S. Lewis Inspirational Writings — The Four Loves*, published in 1991 by Inspirational Press by arrangement with Harcourt Brace Jovanovich Inc, NY, NY.

p. 45 Cecil Rhodes, *The New Book of Knowledge*, volume QR, p. 288, © in 1984 by Grolier Inc., Danbury, CN.

p. 51 Viktor Frankl (1905–1997), Austrian psychiatrist, *Man's Search for Meaning*, 1984, Beacon Press, Boston, MA.

p. 56 Colin Powell, American retired general & secretary of state, 2001–2005, *The Leadership Secrets of Colin Powell* by Oren Harari, © 2002, McGraw Hill Companies.

p. 57 Harvey Mackay, businessman, motivational speaker, www.harveymackay.com.

p. 58 Julia Cameron, teacher, American artist, poet, filmmaker, © 1992, *The Artist's Way: A Spiritual Path to Higher Creativity*, Jeremy P. Tarcher/Pedigee-Putnam Publishing Co., NY, NY.

p. 60 J.R.R. Tolkien, © 1966, The Hobbit, Ballantine Books, NY, NY.

p. 62 John Sculley hired away from Pepsico to work at Apple Inc by Steve Jobs — http://www.pbs.org/wgbh/pages/frontline/president/players/sculley.html

p. 64 Thomas Alva Edison, American businessman and inventor, The New Book of Knowledge, volume E, © 1984 by Grolier, Inc., Danbury, CN.

p. 65 Victor and Mildred Goertzel's *Cradles of Eminence*, 2nd edition updated by Ariel M.W. Hansen and Ted George Goertzel, Ph.D., Great Potential Press, © 2004.

p. 68 Dr. Stephen R. Covey, Leadership authority and teacher, www.stephencovey.com/

p. 68 Florence May Chadwick, *A Fresh Packet of Sower's Seeds* by Fa. Brian Cavanaugh, Paulist Press.

p. 78 Theodore Roosevelt, www.theodorerooseveltassociation.org.